ACHIEVEMENT

A Proven System for Next-Level Growth

DAVID BYRD & MARK SMITH

ISBN: 978-0-9826665-0-0
BUSINESS & ECONOMICS / LEADERSHIP / MOTIVATIONAL

Published by PCG Business, a division of Pilot Communications Group, Inc. 317 Appaloosa Trail Waco, TX 76712
www.thepublishinghub.com

HOW TO REACH DAVID BYRD:
www.davidbyrdconsulting.com

HOW TO REACH MARK SMITH:
www.MyOnlineLeadership.com

HOW TO ORDER:
www.thepublishinghub.com

To everyone who
who wants and needs
to make it to the
next level.

Contents

Introductions

from David Byrd

Achievement is valued in our society because it represents the best in us. It seems as if our Creator placed a divine spark within each of us that drives us to achieve.

Even though achievement seems to be a natural and universal desire, the journey of achievement is usually **elusive** and sometimes **inconsistent**.

Some people strive desperately, only to watch achievement slip through their hands. Almost as a contradiction, achievement seems simple, easy, almost natural for others.

The purpose of this book is to answer the question:

**"Can the basics of achievement
be learned, or is this elusive prize
only for the lucky few?"**

I'll tell you now, achievement can be learned. The truth is, achievement *must* be learned!

Want the "Next Level" of success?

I have invested over 30 years of my life to the study of achievement. Through my associations with the late Paul J.

Meyer for over 30 years and as president of one of his companies, Leadership Management Inc., for over 10 years, and through my leadership consulting, I have worked with top corporate leaders and entrepreneurs at every level.

All these leaders, both past and present, share a common interest. They are leaders who are looking for that "Next-Level" for their organizations and for themselves.

To reach that coveted "Next Level," they must accomplish new goals. They must grow and develop new skills. They must acquire new confidence. They must reach for new levels of awareness.

In short ...
they must
ACHIEVE!

Achievement is a very simple process. **You can achieve by simply doing the right things consistently over a sustained period of time.**

But if achievement is so simple to define, why is achievement not easy for everyone? Good question!

The reality is, as you very well know, achievement is difficult for many people.

I believe that achievement is **not easy** because most people **do not know how to manage the consistency of doing the right things on a daily, moment-by-moment basis.**

You have a strong security blanket!

Daily management from goal-directed focus is difficult because our natural, human instincts fight the growth and change necessary for achievement. The goal of our natural instincts is to keep us safe, and instinctively, we fight for self-preservation.

The no-change, status-quo of life is instinctively interpreted as **security**. We instinctively seek a comfort zone in life where nothing will ever change. The reality is that, although we may desire achievement, we instinctively run from change.

Therein lies the problem.

Most people do not know how to manage the consistency of doing the right things on a daily, moment-by-moment basis

What is needed is a systems approach to achievement, a system that is based on your dreams and goals but separated from the self-imposed limitations of your natural, human instincts. **You need a system that will direct your focus and energy on a daily, moment-by-moment basis.**

In this book, we will outline a proven, systems approach to achievement. This system of achievement involves a development process, which is best communicated in a structured, instructional format. This format has a single purpose: **your measurable results!**

In addition, I am honored to be joined in this book by Mark Smith. He is a dynamic example of achievement and will share his own ideas and real-life examples as confirmation of the validity of the system.

I trust and sincerely hope that this book will serve as guide and counsel for all those who read with a genuine desire to achieve.

— David Byrd

from Mark Smith

David Byrd asks if you are willing to be coachable. Most people say they are, but only 20% are serious ... and only 5% will actually follow through.

When I joined the Navy, I was promptly told, **"Leave all your accomplishments at home. Be coachable."**

So I signed up for everything. I did everything possible. If it was hard or meaningless, I tried it all with an open mind and a heart that was coachable. I didn't prejudge. I was a sponge and learned from everyone.

As a direct result I was awarded the Navy Achievement Medal six times and Sailor Of The Year for 3rd Marine Division. I rose quickly through the ranks. The leaders above me reached down and pulled me up. I was hungry, and they were looking for a few good (and hungry) men!

Truthfully, people join the Navy every day and then count the days until they get out. If you were to interview them, they would be quick to tell you how it was a "waste of time" and how little they did. But in reality, they **didn't take advantage of all resources** that were available to them.

The Navy wanted me to make a career out of it, but I wanted to launch out on my own. I wanted to create something for myself, so with great memories, experiences, and a lot of training from my life in the military, I jumped into civilian life.

8

I now take what I've learned about leadership, work, and effort, and apply that to my business career. I've found it to be incredibly relevant to everything I put my hand to, from selling to leading and from being an entrepreneur to planning my future.

In fact, what I've learned and applied has since made me, and those around me, millions of dollars. My belief is that anyone can do what I did.

Using what I learned

You can learn anywhere, but for me, my learning pad was the Navy. The key to military-style leadership is founded on the core values of honor, courage, and commitment. Everything is based on that core. When the going gets tough, it is so much easier to get through and make things happen because, from day one, everything is based on the sound foundation of core values.

There is also a clear understanding of the mission. You know where you are going, and based on the core values, it's easy to lead.

Leadership is driven down to the lowest level right away. They didn't wait until we were personally developed to start using us. From the start, they taught us how to lead.

In business and in your own pursuit of success and achievement, you also have to start leading right away. You can't wait. If you wait too long, you or someone around you will miss an opportunity. You have to start leading right away.

What's more, if you wait until you feel "ready" or personally developed, you will have effectively slowed everyone else down. If you are leading a team or running a business, you

9

can't wait for someone to be ready to be taught leadership. The time is now to do what needs to be done.

Creating leaders

The military is a leadership factory. That's their secret. They are a factory, and they pump out leaders. Amazingly, they can take young people from every different background, educational level, social level, race, faith, etc., and they turn them into leaders.

Their secret is to develop the masses, driving leadership down to the lowest level. They create an environment of achievement, and people make big steps forward because the environment breeds leadership and achievement.

It starts with bite-sized pieces, developing them from the get-go, and putting into their minds that they will achieve greatness.

When you are set up for success, you are much more likely to succeed.

Another part of the military's success in creating leaders is that their system is duplicable. The mantra is to **watch** one, **do** one, **teach** one.

If you want to achieve big things, they don't want to hear about it. They simply want you to **be coachable** and to **plug into the system**, a proven system that has decades and decades of leadership ahead of you.

You plug into the system, you get instruction, you do it, and then you teach it. People get to see what success and achievement looks like. When you see what it looks like, and there is a system in place, it's easier to accomplish great things.

I always say that one hour in the field is equal to 10 hours in the classroom. There is nothing better than actually doing and experiencing something. You have to get your hands dirty, and when you do, you'll truly "get it," and you'll be able to teach it to others.

The pinnacle of achievement in leadership is teaching another person. If you aren't duplicating your efforts, then you've failed. What's more, if you teach five other people, and they don't teach anyone else, then everything you taught will eventually die. You must duplicate yourself, and those you teach must do the same. That is how you grow and multiply.

I have led many people in my military career and in my business career. I learned that I could never judge people on the outside, but in a short amount of time, based on their actions, I could tell who was an achiever and who was not.

My hope, belief, and prayer is that you will choose to be an achiever!

— Mark Smith

PART I

Choosing
to Succeed

How many times have you heard that success is a choice? We all have, and success is a choice ... but if we don't know what to do, how can we choose?

Chapters 1-4 focus on the very elements that make up the necessary choices for achievement and success. Upon reading those chapters, you will know exactly what to do with those future choices that lead to achievement.

Chapter One

Choice — The Foundation of Achievement

Achievement is simply the result of doing the "right things" consistently over a sustained period of time. Doing the "right things" is a direct result of your personal choice. Your future is built on the choices you make, day by day, moment by moment.

It is a **natural, human tendency** to disregard the importance of your everyday choices. I think we minimize the importance of our choices because the consequences of those choices are delayed.

**We do not experience
immediate results
from most of our choices.**

If we did, we **certainly would be more selective** with our choices!

Instead, we are free to make a bad or ineffective choice and feel no immediate impact, leaving us with the impression that no harm has been done.

13

We have all watched superstar athletes at the heights of their careers, on top of the world, suddenly make a very bad choice that later brings down everything they have worked for. We ask, "Why did they do that?"

The answer is simple: **They thought they could get away with it.** All of us would make better decisions if there were immediate consequences to our choices.

For example, if you immediately gained 50 pounds every time you ate a single bowl of ice cream, you would never eat another bowl of ice cream again. What's more, ice cream companies would be out of business by tomorrow morning!

But that is **not** the way it works.

Here is the reality:

> You eat a bowl of ice cream and nothing happens immediately. Ice cream taste good, so you decide to eat two bowls tomorrow, three the next day, and so on. Six months later you step onto the scales and find that you have gained 50 pounds. Your response is, "Why have I gained 50 pounds? I'm shocked!"

The 50 pounds came from your **daily choices** about ice cream. The consequences of bad choices accumulated gradually without your noticing it. You can, of course, choose to stop eating ice cream daily, and in six months, lose the extra 50 pounds.

This is an exaggerated example of how choice is directly related to long-term results, and **you should never be shocked with your results because you are in complete**

control. You are not a victim. The quality of your life is all about your choices.

Every day you make thousands of choices. You enjoy the freedom to choose your thoughts, perspectives, actions, and associations. **However, each choice you make in life has a consequence.** So, by filling your days with effective choices, you build a future of beneficial consequences. What that means is this:

> **The quality of your choices**
> **will determine the quality**
> **of your life.**

The Achievement System

The foundation of any system of achievement is learning to make effective, daily choices. Surprisingly, this is a unique ability. We do not naturally possess the capacity of making consistent, effective choices!

Why?

Before we answer that question, it is necessary to understand what effective choice is. **Effective choice is defined as those choices that directly relate to your immediate goals.** For instance, if we continue with the ice cream example previously used, the choice of eating too much ice cream simply because it tastes good is an instinctive, ineffective choice if health and weight control is your goal.

However, the choice of limiting the excessive intake of calories from ice cream is an effective choice directly related to the goal of maximizing your health. Therefore, **effective choices are goal-directed choices, not instinctive choices.**

15

Now, back to the question first posed:

**Why do we NOT naturally
possess the capacity
to make consistent effective choices
related to our achievement?**

FROM THE DESK OF MARK SMITH:

You need to have a white-hot, burning desire inside of you, and in order to have this white-hot desire, you have to identify a motivator within you. You can't buy a program to be motivated. You can't go to a weekend seminar to be motivated. Motivation comes from within. External things can help fuel and guide you, but the motivation has to come from inside of you.

Identify what is the most important thing to you. If you want more time with your family, then that is your motivator. That's your goal, your "why" for doing what you do.

To help fuel your burning desire, you have to spend time in self-talk to define what you want, but without a specific target, you'll miss it. You have to be specific. Clearly define, vividly imagine. You have to have it. Nothing else will work for you unless you have an internal intensity or burning desire.

If someone were to hold your head under water right now, you would have some oxygen in your system. About 30 seconds from now, you'll be highly motivated to get some oxygen. At 60 seconds, you'll go through a brick wall to get that oxygen!

When you have to have something, and you'll do whatever it takes to get it, that's how intense your burning desire needs to be. But if your desire is not that intense, all the distractions of life will get in your way, all the potholes will derail you, and the speed bumps will become mountains.

Find your motivator, now!

The answer is both simple and complex.

Your natural, human instincts have one goal for you: **your safety**. Your instincts really do not care about your goals, only about your safety and comfort. When you manage your daily activities from your natural, human instincts, your response will always be in favor of keeping you where you are.

Your brain interprets status-quo as security.

It's natural to stay right where you are.
Your brain interprets sameness or status-quo as security.

In short:

> your instincts are fighting **AGAINST** your achievement because achievement always involves **CHANGE** and growth, both of which are **CONTRARY** to sameness.

This means that you are undermining your own success and achievement ... naturally!

To achieve, you must first learn to **intentionally manage your process of making effective choices**, and that process must be systematic rather than instinctive.

This works because ...

> **A systems approach to achievement bypasses your natural instincts.**

Read that a few times to let the words digest.

I have worked with clients who have spent their entire lives managing achievement instinctively with sporadic results. On the other hand, I have watched overwhelming results from leaders who manage by a proven system of achievement.

The ultimate purpose of this book is to help you understand **Your instincts really do not care about your goals.** and implement a proven system of achievement. That system begins with learning to make effective choices now, and every day. Effective choices lead to effective actions, which in turn lead to beneficial results.

If you understand this system, **you can learn how to achieve!**

Results can be directly traced back to a point of origin: **your choices!** Choice builds the foundation of your future achievement. **Your first step toward achievement is learning to make effective choices on a consistent, daily basis.** If there is such a thing as a secret to achievement, a significant part of that secret is ...

**being aware of the power
of your choices and
learning to choose
effectively!**

Qualifying factors of achievement

Sustained achievement usually depends upon certain qualifying factors. The following is a list of four qualifying factors, along with a question for each.

By answering each of the following questions, you can determine if you have the underlying, emotional foundation for sustained achievement.

1) Commitment to a goal — Do I have a burning desire to achieve something specific?

2) Courage to persevere — Am I willing to follow a system in developing an enhanced level of emotional courage?

3) Open-mindedness — Am I willing to be coached without being defensive?

4) Accountable for your actions — Will I choose to be accountable for my effective actions?

FROM THE DESK OF MARK SMITH:

Line up high achievers, and you'll see that each one of them has a system. They all have a daily methodology to get them from day to day, month to month, and year to year.

Some may not be aware of it, but if you were to observe them, you would see that each one of them has a systematic approach to get things done.

Without a system, every distraction will get you off track. High achievers, on the other hand, can take the biggest distractions of life, such as layoffs, death, betrayal, disappointments, bankruptcy, and still keep going.

There is simply no other option. Achievers will look for ways to get over it, get around it, or go under it. They will get it done, regardless, and they do ... because they have a system.

You must have a system.

Looking at these qualifying factors, it is important to know this principle:

> **There can be no achievement**
> **without these characteristics**
> **or without a willingness to**
> **develop these characteristics.**

You are your own boss

I have invested over 30 years of my life in working with people in leadership positions. From my work, I have discovered that leadership skills are necessary for **everyone** and are not exclusively reserved for those who have been appointed to leadership positions.

The reality is that you are the CEO of your life!

You are responsible for your results. No one else can make the choices that you must make for your life. **Your life today represents the cumulative impact of the choices you have made, and your future will represent the sum of your choices from today forward.** You cannot change the past, but you can dramatically impact your future.

Except in extreme cases, circumstances have played a very small role in your current life position. I know this is a hard concept for some to accept, but I have found it to be true.

FROM THE DESK OF MARK SMITH:

Are you willing to be coachable? If you haven't had success, then what you've been doing has probably not been working. If you are truly on a path of achievement, then regardless of your past, learn and be coachable.

The truth is that culture, environment, and circumstances can dictate your future ... **but only if you choose to allow it**.

It is **still** your choice!

Some believe that if circumstances were perfect, they would be able to achieve. Others wait for the right circumstances to come along. My experience with high achievers proves the opposite. High achievers have difficult circumstances, just like everyone else, but they **consistently respond with positive actions rather than negative beliefs**.

It is your choice to become a victim of your circumstances or to respond to your circumstances with effective actions. History is filled with stories of those who have overcome unimaginable circumstances simply by choosing to do so.

Culture, environment, and circumstances can dictate your future ... but only if you choose to allow it.

Reading this book could be your first step toward building a future of your design, or you may be seeking to enhance your already successful journey. Regardless of your current position in life, your future **will always be determined** by the quality of your choices.

Notes to Self:

Chapter Two

Managing the Choice of Attitude

As you know, the foundation of achievement is learning to make effective choices. Since each of us makes thousands of choices daily, it is vitally important that we make the right choices.

In all the choices you make, there are three major areas, or choice categories, that will determine the degree of your future achievement: the choice of **attitude**, the choice of **action**, and the choice of **accountability**.

We will devote separate chapters to each of these critical categories because your effective management of these three life choices **is vital to your future achievement**. In this chapter, we will discuss one of these top three choices — the choice of attitude.

Attitude is a choice!

Your management of a consistent and productive, positive attitude will determine the degree of your future achievement.

It sounds so simple, but managing a consistent, effective attitude will be one of the greatest challenges of your life. In my career, I have experienced only a few people who, in my opinion, have done an effective job at this.

Why is attitude management so difficult?

That's simple ... **FEAR!**

The emotion of fear is a protective reflex and is a basic, instinctive, human response. As an example, if you see or feel a perceived danger, your natural response is fear. **Because fear is instinctive, many people naturally develop the habit of responding to most of the circumstances of life from the emotion of fear.** Unfortunately, this leads to negative, unproductive attitudes.

> **Managing a consistent, effective attitude will be one of the greatest challenges of your life.**

Yes, negative attitudes are natural, human responses!

Every news channel knows that negative news tends to appeal to our natural, human instincts. That is why approximately 80% of the news reported is either negative or communicated with a negative slant. The unfortunate truth here is this:

We are more comfortable
with negative news
than with positive news.

So, managing a positive, effective attitude is difficult because it is neither natural nor instinctive. **You must DEVELOP the capacity to manage a positive attitude.**

This leads me to my point: **We all need a systems approach to attitude management.** Without it, we will be subject to our natural, instinctive, negative thinking.

To develop a system of attitude management, you first need to understand the mechanics of how negative attitudes are developed.

Negative attitudes are instinctive

The average person develops and maintains negative thinking habits, and it all comes about instinctively!

Remember, your natural, human instincts are concerned only with you safety and comfort, and in order to keep you

---

FROM THE DESK OF MARK SMITH:

Waking up in the morning with a positive mental attitude is entirely up to you. It's an attitude of not letting anything bother you, even though you really control very little in life.

You can choose the right associations, but life brings you a lot of curve balls. Your attitude will get you through, which makes having the right mindset an absolute necessity.

What will give someone the right attitude? I've found that in achievement, the end result needs to cast such a large shadow over the person wanting to achieve that it causes him or her to be positive all the time.

Why are you chasing a goal? What is it that is bigger than your financial goal? If it totally fires you up and gets you going, then you are going to be laser focused on reaching your goal ... and you will be positive as a result. All the negative stuff that just happens will not get you off track because your vision is so big.

Find a big enough vision, and you will be an unflinching, unstoppable, positive person!

---

safe, your established habit of thinking must be maintained, and that is why the negative-thinking habit of pessimism is so common. Instinctively, **your brain interprets pessimism as a protective mechanism of security**, and your habit of pessimism is reinforced constantly.

Think of it this way:

> If you are skeptical of **everyone** and **everything**, your human instincts interpret that habit as a **safe comfort zone from all risks**.

However, the habitual perspective of pessimism will eventually become a comfortable thinking habit, and that leads to unproductive habits of thought.

In other words, you develop negative attitudes. Upon these ineffective thinking habits you begin to build "comfort zones" for yourself that impede your own growth.

Comfort zones

A comfort zone is an emotional mindset that is created from your thinking habits over a period of time. These comfort zones **misrepresent** the position of security. Your emotions interpret fear as a threat, and you then naturally retreat to your comfort zone where nothing is going to change. That status quo position is instinctively interpreted as safety.

To grow, you must develop your potential, and that potential always lies just beyond your comfort zones.

Of course, the emotional security represented by a comfort zone is an illusion. It offers no security at all, but it feels emotionally comfortable because it has been built on thinking habits that are motivated by fear.

For example, the following statements represent just a few of the more common expressions of well-established comfort zones:

"I don't trust anyone."

"I'm secure as long as I have my job."

"I don't like risks."

"If I try something new, I might fail."

"I worry about what other people may think of me."

"They have a lot of money; they sure are lucky."

Everyone has comfort zones — and you do, too. **Your comfort zones serve no purpose other than prohibiting your own growth.**

Here's the truth:

**You cannot grow
and be comfortable
at the same time.**

Growth feels uncomfortable because it pushes you out of your comfort zones. To grow, you must develop your potential, and that potential always lies just beyond your comfort zones.

Attitude management is imperative for every person at every level of achievement. Regardless of your level of

27

achievement or degree of success, **there is never a position in life** where you can forget to manage your thinking habits.

Managing a positive attitude

I have heard positive attitude described as a "soft skill" and therefore not considered to be a significant factor in achievement. I strongly disagree. **Most dysfunction in business and personal achievement can be traced back to a root cause: ineffective thinking habits!**

It does not have to be that way. You can learn to manage your habits of thought and directly affect your level of performance and achievement.

Effective change always begins with awareness. People will choose to change when they are aware that the change will serve their best interest!

So, the first step in growth is becoming aware, for with an enhanced level of awareness, you can make choices that promote positive attitudes.

FROM THE DESK OF MARK SMITH:

You absolutely cannot associate with negative people. If you have negative tendencies, you will attract negative people. And then, as you start to become negative, the positive people in your life will leave you. After all, positive people only want to be with other positive people.

This alone is bad enough, but you start to gain more and more negative associations, and it spirals down from there. In the end, negativity attracts negative people and repels positive people. You lose twice!

The answer is simple: Don't hang out with negative people!

What is attitude?

An attitude can best be defined as a **habit of thought**. You naturally develop certain patterns of thinking about the people and world around you. These thinking habits can be conditioned and patterned by parents, friends, culture, environment, experiences, and circumstances.

If you do not assume personal responsibility for developing your own effective, positive attitudes, the world around you will shape your attitudes with average thinking, which is usually negative and unproductive. As a result, you become a victim of your own ineffective thinking patterns.

A good working definition of positive attitude is this:

> **a predetermined habit of thought dominated by faith, hope, and positive expectancy.**

The long-term result of a consistent, positive attitude is fulfillment and achievement. Without question, the long-term benefits of maintaining a positive attitude are far more desirable than the long-term effects of a negative attitude.

Every thought you entertain during the day is either positive or negative. There is no in-between or neutral thought. Every moment of your thinking pattern during the day either serves your growth or serves your stagnation.

The fastest way to promote achievement is to believe it to be possible.

Many people describe their attitude as neutral, neither positive nor negative. However, since everything in nature is either growing or decaying, there can be no neutral positions. You and your thoughts are alive and dynamic.

29

The thinking patterns that determine your attitudes either ...

**work to bring about your growth
or work to bring about
your decline.**

It truly is that simple!

Thoughts are creative

A positive attitude fosters creativity. Creativity cannot exist in negative thought. For example, it is impossible to discover a creative solution by thinking about all the impossibilities. **Your mind cannot entertain creativity and negative thought at the same time.**

To find a creative solution, you must think in terms of the possibilities rather than the impossibilities. The fastest way to promote achievement is to believe it to be possible. That requires the management of a consistent, positive attitude.

If you allow your natural responses of fear to direct your thinking, you personally sabotage your opportunities for achievement by choosing to quit or not to act.

Clearly, you want the long-term benefits of managing a positive attitude. We all do! Therefore, understand that **intentionally choosing to maintain an effective, positive attitude will be your most significant lesson in life.** Your daily management of the choice of attitude, on a moment-by-moment basis, is a key element in your future achievement.

The enemy of positive thought

Everyone is challenged by the emotion of fear. Fear is a

natural, human emotion that instinctively causes us to respond with a defensive reflex to any perceived threat.

If left unmanaged, **your attitudes will be controlled** by the emotion of fear.

For example, if you set a goal that requires you to do new things, these new activities will seem uncomfortable at first.

FROM THE DESK OF MARK SMITH:

Achievement is 80% mental. Everything in my life that I wanted badly enough, even back as a little kid, I pursued with self-talk. Society tells us not to waste our time talking to ourselves (daydreaming), but people are so quick to feed us their negative words that rattle around in our brains for years.

You might have heard:

- "You'll never amount to anything."
- "You were born on the wrong side of the tracks."
- "You can't do it."

Instead of believing these lies, you need to decide for yourself which words you will listen to. I have chosen to live life with positive expectancy, and my self-talk lines up accordingly.

When some people call me, I refuse to let their negativity dump on me. There is only one sale that is ever made: You either sell them or they sell you. I refuse to let non-achievers sell me. Instead, I sell them.

Are there incredible things that you want to accomplish some day? Are they realistic? Maybe not, but don't let that stop you.

Do you aim high and miss high? Or do you aim low and miss low? The achiever is still an achiever. Achievers are shooting for the stars ... and they land on the moon. Others shoot for the curb ... and end up in the gutter.

That is normal, but you may instinctively respond with fearful feelings because the new activities are uncomfortable. You psychologically interpret those fearful feelings as "risks" or "dangers," while in fact these new activities may not be dangerous at all ... **but you will naturally respond with negative feelings**.

We all have a basic fear of risks and the unknown. This response is natural, yet absolutely counterproductive to achievement. **All achievement requires you to grow beyond your current status or position.**

You cannot possibly expect to grow and not confront new activities, skills, and responsibilities. If you allow your natural responses of fear to direct your thinking, you personally sabotage your opportunities for achievement by choosing to quit or not to act.

Most of the people who fail to achieve did not fail at all. They simply allowed fear to control their thinking and quit. The fear of risk and the unknown were stronger than their desire to achieve.

5 steps to mental toughness

There are five steps that will help you develop the mental toughness needed to face the challenge of your natural instinct of fear ... and to win!

STEP #1 — Maintain positive expectancy

You must keep the vision of your desired, future achievement in the forefront of your mental focus. Keep your eye on the prize! Also, recognize that fear **serves no purpose** in your personal growth unless you are actually physically threatened.

Achievement is 80% mental! **You will first accomplish your dreams in your mind before you ever realize them materially.** Being "rich" or "accomplished" is first a state of mind.

Build a vision of your future that is stronger than your fears, and fill your thinking patterns with positive expectancy.

Positive expectancy acts as a magnet. **You attract to yourself that which you set out for yourself.** Your positive expectancy actually attracts the circumstances that you will need to realize your achievement.

STEP #2 — Manage your daily choices according to your goals, not your feelings

Managing consistent, positive expectancy is difficult because you never feel the same, physically or emotionally, every single day of the week. If you only work on your goals when you feel good, **your actions will be too inconsistent to produce results**.

My long-time friend and mentor, Paul J. Meyer, would say, "Follow through with your daily plans regardless of circumstances or what other people say, think, or do."

In other words, your dreams for the future must be strong enough to keep you following through with those plans on a daily basis, no matter how you feel.

STEP #3 — Aggressively manage your positive relationships

Your associations with others will either promote your growth or deter it. The thinking habits of those with whom you associate affect your thinking. You must, therefore, foster relationships with people who inspire and influence your growth.

You will attract to yourself that which you set out for yourself. If you are positive and goal-directed, you will attract those of similar thinking habits.

Aggressively avoid those who impose their negative beliefs or attitudes on you. Negative attitudes create negative energy that affects all those in association. You cannot

FROM THE DESK OF MARK SMITH:

High achievers have an innate ability to believe in things that are not yet produced, done, or completed. Look at all the different businesses in the world and the people who led them. Henry Ford is a great example. He had belief in a system that didn't yet exist! He had faith and made car production a reality.

Farmers are the same way. They plant the seeds and they believe that they will reap a harvest. You never see farmers out in the fields, yelling at the ground or begging seeds to grow. Farmers believe in the process. They know that with water, dirt, and sunlight, the seeds will grow. The process works, and they follow it.

Bamboo may take years to generate good roots, but it can grow 2 feet in a single day! No farmer would expect such results 24 hours after planting anything, but many people often do when they get started in a new business or opportunity!

Having faith in a proven system is what I call "blind faith," and it's not misplaced. It's what is needed. A new farmer doesn't question the seed-growing process — he just goes with it, on faith.

High achievers have faith in a process, and if you are new to working with high achievers, have faith in their leadership. Follow them. Recognize that it's an achievement process. You just need to follow it.

engage in negative relationships without being negatively affected, so you must manage your personal relationships aggressively!

STEP #4 — Live in the moment!

Life comes to each of us one day at a time. You cannot live in the future any more than you can change the past. The past is gone and tomorrow does not exist.

Many people never succeed in their life plans because they are always saying, "I'll start tomorrow." Tomorrow turns into next week, next month, and next year. Some call it procrastination, but in reality, **it is nothing more than a comfort zone**.

You procrastinate on your personal growth because it is simply more comfortable to wait. The decision to wait is most often a decision to not grow and to stay in your comfort zone.

The only part of living that really matters is right now ... this moment.

**Living in the past
or worrying about tomorrow
is wasteful and of no importance.**

Learn to live right now! Change your thinking about waiting and develop the attitude of urgency in applying effective actions daily.

STEP #5 — Believe

Faith is a spiritual term. It makes no sense intellectually and can be understood only from a spiritual perspective.

Regardless of your religious or non-religious position, belief is vital in your growth and achievement, and you cannot understand belief without an understanding of faith.

A good definition of faith is being sure of what you hope for and certain of what you do not see. You now understand why I said that it makes no sense intellectually, but faith and belief **in your potential to achieve** is vital.

Psychologists suggest that we all have three dominant parts of our being: physical, mental, and spiritual. You cannot grow and achieve without the basic belief that you can do it, and that belief involves faith. Faith requires a spiritual perspective.

Some cannot believe in anything that they cannot see or touch, but growth is always unseen until it is achieved.

There will be times in your achievement journey when quitting or giving up will seem like the only alternatives. At these times, it will take the strength of your faith to prevail. **You must believe that you can achieve, for it is the spark that sustains you.**

Managing your positive attitude

Armed with a new level of awareness of how and why negative attitudes are instinctive, you now understand why a positive attitude development program is vital to your growth, success, and achievement.

You must develop a positive, productive attitude. It will never happen naturally, **but just because it is not natural does NOT mean you cannot do it!**

36

Notes to Self:

Chapter Three

Managing the Choice of Action

The choice of action is the second of the big three (attitude, action, accountability) life choices that form the foundation of achievement.

Let me ask you this:

If a key component of achievement is "doing the right things," then what are the "right things"?

The "right things" are those predetermined, effective actions that are **necessary** in achieving your goals.

Just like the choice of attitude, action is a choice, and the choices regarding your effective actions require your consistent, daily management. Every day you choose your activities. Those activities will either be effective or ineffective.

How can you determine whether an action is **effective** or **ineffective**? Simply by the end result. What you did, did it work or not? Effective actions ALWAYS **deliver desirable results!**

Effective actions

In my experiences working with high achievers, I find a common misconception regarding the choice of action. Many high achievers **overwhelm themselves** with more than they can do and then "beat themselves up" for not getting it all done.

This behavior becomes a vicious cycle of anxious, over-optimistic planning and feelings of defeat or failure.

Effective actions always deliver desirable results! What's interesting is that this behavior becomes a comfort zone for many! They are never satisfied because they feel they can never do enough, and this becomes a pattern of thinking and pattern of action.

Here is a key to understanding the choice of action:

> **It's not how much you do,**
> **but the effectiveness of**
> **what you do**
> **that really counts!**

Effective actions are those predetermined activities that support the accomplishment of your goals.

Ineffective actions, on the other hand, are those activities that tend to fill up the daily schedule but are not related to your goals. They are usually things that need to be done but are not directly related to your achievement.

For example, the dishwasher needs emptying and the car needs to be washed, but neither will advance your future vision of financial independence.

People who achieve greatly have a unique ability of separating the necessary to-do items (i.e. washing the car, balancing the checkbook, cleaning the office, etc.) **from the necessary, effective actions required to accomplish a goal.** They understand that both types of actions are necessary, but they never confuse the two in planning their day.

The underlying foundation of achievement is the consistency of your daily, effective actions.

> **Great achievers have a unique ability to separate the necessary to-do items from the necessary effective actions required to accomplish a goal.**

If left unmanaged, your natural tendency is to allow your day to be managed by your fears and comfort zones. The danger of following your human instincts in choosing your daily activities is that there is no distinguishing attention paid to those actions that hold the **highest payoff**.

This mindset leads you to believe that the necessary items on your to-do list are just as important as the necessary effective actions that help you reach your goals, **and nothing could be further from the truth!**

This is precisely why people choose not to do the high payoff actions. They are instinctively drawn toward those activities that are most comfortable.

Building confidence
Admittedly, the most effective actions are usually not the most comfortable activities. And if you are working on

building confidence in a new skill, what are the odds that you will naturally choose to work on your new skill rather than choose to be comfortable?

Close to zero. And that is precisely my point! **You will not do what you need to do.**

Developing confidence in a new skill requires practicing something that you have never done before. In fact, you develop confidence from the experience of successful attempts. You try something, it works, and you have more confidence for the next attempt.

The experience is usually uncomfortable. Everything within us wants to revert back to our normal routine.

**When we experience discomfort,
we instinctively seek
to return to a
more comfortable
activity.**

Your natural, human instincts are designed to measure the quality of your comfort level and safety, not the degree of your achievement. To achieve, **you must manage your choice of action from a proven system** rather than from your feelings or emotions.

Effective actions are related to the **desired end result**, and you must always **measure your results** related to your goals.

Identifying effective actions

Not only is it essential for you to understand the effectiveness of your actions, but it is critical for you to become proficient at identifying those actions.

Within every discipline of industry or field of work, certain indicators of achievement can be identified. Those indicators are defined by the **significance of their contributions** to your success.

For example, a car dealership has the ultimate responsibility of selling cars at a profit in sufficient numbers so that the profit from total sales is greater than the overhead and payroll of operations on a monthly basis.

We can identify the "indicators of success" by first understanding that the goal of selling a sufficient number of cars on a monthly basis is the desired end result. Given the goal, we can then break the process of selling cars down into the key indicators of performance, or KPIs (key performance indicators).

To achieve, you must manage your choice of action from a proven system rather than from your feelings or emotions.

New cars are purchased by people who are interested in a new car, have the ability to make a decision, and have the money to buy. That defines a qualified prospect.

The process of selling a car always begins with a qualified prospect, and qualified prospects are developed through a number of leads that come through a series of advertisements and call lists.

From this simple analysis, we now can identify each KPI:
> #1 — effective advertising
> #2 — call lists
> #3 — developing call lists into interested buyers
> #4 — developing interested buyers into qualified prospects
> #5 — appointments to show cars to qualified prospects

If these five KPIs are performed effectively in sufficient numbers, the end result will be car sales. This, of course, is a simplified example for the purpose of demonstration.

Any achievement goal can be broken into the key indicators of performance using this same system. When you know the right things (KPIs) that define goal-directed effectiveness, it is easier to manage your effective actions. What this means is:

**You can now design your daily actions
around the KPIs in sufficient numbers
to hit your desired goals.**

As you know, achievement is the process of doing the right things consistently over a sustained period of time. In other

---

FROM THE DESK OF MARK SMITH:

Many of the processes of achievement are simple. It's human nature, however, to not like simple things. Why? Because there is nothing to hide from. People want the complicated way to do things so they can have an excuse to fail.

In my business, we have a very straightforward duplicable system that works. But when you add new people to the system, they try to come up with a million ways to do it, and they complicate it. That is why I tell people, "You are always one step away from ruining your system."

In most processes or businesses, the longest distance from one point to another is usually a shortcut. Did you catch that?

Adding new steps and shortcuts are really long-cuts in the end. They slow you down. You don't get traction.

People who are not fully coachable have not gained belief in the process. They try to complicate things instead of just doing what is simple. Be coachable. Keep it simple. And win!

---

words, with KPIs in mind, **achievement happens moment by moment, one day at a time!** When you know the right things to do, and you have identified the key performance indicators, simply exercise your power of choice and consistently do the right things.

You now understand the significance of effective actions, how to identify the KPIs that define effective actions, and the significance of the power of choice in managing your effective actions.

It takes approximately 90 days of practice to begin to actually see your new planning habit begin to work.

Your goal now is to begin to build the habit of planning and managing your effective actions moment by moment, one day at a time, by a specific and proven achievement system.

The results will astound you!

Your two life choices

You only have two choices in life: **grow or decline!** There is no in-between position in life. Your human instincts will *always* direct you toward safety by consistently encouraging you to stay where you are and to not change.

If you choose achievement, you must build the habit of planning and managing your daily actions by a proven system. Your human instincts will not be sufficient.

This is no easy task, and I have found that it takes consistent practice to develop this habit. It takes approximately 90 days of practice to begin to actually see your new planning habit begin to work. **It is not easy to bypass your human**

instincts. It takes constant diligence and focus to stay on track.

In developing this habit of personal management, never beat yourself up over forgetting a day here and there. That is natural and happens to everyone. When you find yourself off track and going back to your old comfort zones, stop and immediately get back to your proven system.

Measuring your effective actions

Remember that it is important to manage your effective actions in sufficient numbers to accomplish your goal. This requires that you measure your KPIs by what we call a "benchmark."

A benchmark is a time-proven standard for each KPI that, when performed at that level of activity, will produce a given degree of achievement.

Take another look at the car dealership example. The dealer must sell a certain number of cars monthly to produce the desired level of profitability. Let's say that the dealership must sell 20 cars each month to hit its goal, and from past experience the dealer knows that it takes 60 qualified prospects with a 33% closing average to sell 20 cars.

Lagging indicators track what has already happened. It's too late at that point, you can't do anything about it. The answer is to track leading indicators.

So, the benchmark for monthly qualified prospects is 60. If the dealership has 10 sales professionals, each salesperson would have a benchmark of 8 qualified prospects per month. Suppose each salesperson delivers 8 qualified prospects a month, the dealership would have a flow of 80 qualified prospects, which is more than enough to hit the goal of 20 car sales.

Using this system, you can determine the benchmark for each KPI for your own efforts. **The benchmarks must be based on experience**, and if you have no experience with your business, find someone with experience to help you determine your benchmarks.

By measuring your benchmark for each KPI monthly, you can develop a six-month rolling average. From this average, you can predict **_with accuracy_** your future degree of achievement.

This type of activity measurement is called a "leading indicator" of future business. Many business leaders simply measure and track monthly sales, which is what we call a "lagging indicator."

FROM THE DESK OF MARK SMITH:

You are the only variable. There is nothing you cannot accomplish when you refuse to be your own excuse.

I have seen people who have time, ability, and motivation fail to achieve because they were not willing to take personal responsibility along the way.

Are you willing to do everything it takes when nobody is looking? And when nobody is looking, what's your attitude? What are you doing? What's your process?

High achievers are always working on it. They don't need to be watched or micromanaged. They have a sense of honor. They will get it done. It's an all day, every day mentality.

Are you willing to do what it takes to succeed? You are your only variable.

Lagging indicators track what has already happened, which means you **cannot apply any corrective actions** because the problem has already happened.

However, **by tracking leading indicators**, you have time to take corrective actions and avoid a future decline in desired results because you are measuring the *predictors* of future results.

Choosing, identifying, managing, and measuring your effective actions is the key to consistent achievement: doing the right things consistently over a sustained period of time.

Managing the choice of action is a vital part of your system of achievement.

Notes to Self:

Chapter Four

Managing the Choice of Accountability

All of us stand at the crossroads of thousands of daily choices, but one of the most effective choices you will ever make regarding achievement is the choice of accountability.

The choice of accountability is the third of the big three (attitude, action, accountability) life choices that form the foundation of achievement.

Most people cringe whenever the word "accountability" is used. It reminds us of the time when we had to do something that we did not want to do, or the time when we had to report to someone we did not respect. **But that is not the context** of this discusion of accountability.

Accountability is motivational force

From this point on, I want you to think of accountability as **a motivational force that will push you beyond your self-imposed limitations**. And THAT is a very good thing!

51

Achievement is about moving to the next level of life, about doing things you never dreamed possible. To achieve, you must change, and change is adverse to our basic human instincts. This means that:

**You must use all of your
creative gifts of imagination,
intuition, and choice
to counterbalance your
instinctive responses to change.**

Your human instincts were designed and built into your mental makeup specifically to keep you safe. It accomplishes its objective by encouraging you to seek a comfort zone where nothing ever changes.

Psychologically, your brain instinctively views growth and change **as a threat** and immediately encourages you to retreat to more comfortable activities. **That is why unproductive habits are so difficult to change!** It is also why mediocrity is the norm, and achievement is the exception.

It is important to seek an "outside-in" perspective to bring about the kind of change you need for sustainable achievement and growth. This perspective can come from a mentor or group of people with like-minded interests to whom you choose to be accountable for your goals.

The choice of accountability is usually the most significant choice anyone can make regarding their future achievement.

The choice of accountability is usually **the most significant choice anyone can make** regarding their future achievement.

How accountability works

In making the choice of accountability, it is important to understand the mechanics of how and why it works.

You remember the simple formula for achievement: doing the right things consistently over a sustained period of time.

To make your choice of accountability more effective, you must identify the "right things," which we call key performance indicators or KPIs. At every level of achievement there are always certain activities that must be consistently performed for achievement to take place. Looking at the history of previous achievers is a good place to start.

The next step in making the choice of accountability is finding someone who has achieved at the level to which you aspire. Once you learn the right things to do from that person, **you need to discover the level of activity required to achieve your goal** within the time frame of your target date. This standard level of activity, as you know, is your "benchmark."

Now, with that understood, let's define achievement more effectively.

**Achievement is performing
all the required KPIs,
at benchmark, consistently
over a sustained period of time.**

That is how you achieve — you **choose to be accountable to your desired level of KPIs at benchmark**. That is the key to your effectiveness.

The 3 parts of accountability

There are three parts of accountability that seem to hold true. The following describes these parts.

#1 — Making a commitment

When you are striving to achieve, commitment takes on a whole different meaning. I have seen more commitments broken than commitments kept. This seems to be average behavior within our society.

The foundation for winning behavior is keeping your commitments.

High achievers, however, act differently. They develop what I call a "winning behavior," and the foundation for winning behavior is this: *keeping commitments*. It is evident by their habit of always doing what they say they are going to do.

When you choose to be accountable to your goals, you must:

A) make a commitment to perform the KPIs at a level you can perform and

B) report on that performance weekly to a mentor or a group of like-minded people.

Performing at benchmark, in the beginning, is not the most important issue. The most important issue is to **do what you say you are going to do**. The difference between what you say and what you do is called your **performance gap**.

Your objective is to do what you say and consistently increase your performance until you reach benchmark.

FROM THE DESK OF MARK SMITH:

The biggest curse word in achievement is "accountability," but I believe accountability is a required ingredient for success.

I spend a lot of time helping people improve their lives, businesses, and futures, and for those who have not yet achieved the level of success they want, my first step with them is to set up some sort of accountability relationship with them.

It might be:

- a weekly call to check in on their goals,
- a time management system to keep them on target, or
- a simple sheet of paper on which they track their efforts.

Interestingly, what I have found is that with more than 80% of people, when we implement accountability, we both learn that they simply are not doing the work! It isn't a lack of knowledge, inferior education, needing a better business partner, the wrong opportunity, or anything else.

They are just not doing the work!

Instead, they are busy trying to find shortcuts or ways to complicate the system. Some may try to avoid the issue, shuffle papers, and try to do other busywork, but usually it comes down to people not doing what they committed to do.

If the work required or system is simple, people can't hide or claim that it was "too difficult" to do. You hold them accountable. Let them look in the mirror and see their own reflection. They have to step up and take responsibility for their own actions.

If they want to be the leader they need to be, if they want to reach the next level, and if they want to reach the goals they dream about, then doing the necessary actions is the answer — and through accountability, they can do just that!

When all the layers of the onion have been peeled back, accountability is the most raw element of personal achievement.

The time it takes you to get to benchmark is completely up to you.

I have used this affirmation for years regarding commitment: **"A commitment made is a debt unpaid until delivered."**

Some people make commitments and then decide if they are really going to follow through.

Consistent growth requires confidence, and confidence only comes from the experience of successful attempts.

For me, a commitment made is like owing money, and I have signed the note! I cannot forfeit on that commitment any more than I can forfeit on borrowed money.

Doing what you say you are going to do is the most important winner behavior you will ever develop, and the choice of accountability helps you develop that behavior.

#2 — Building confidence in your untapped potential

Most people do not develop in grand leaps. Occasionally you will see a top achiever quickly rise to the top, but I have experienced that most of us grow in small increments.

The reality of achievement **is that it does not matter how small the step is, as long as you take those steps consistently and those steps continue to increase**. It is the old grow or decline theory. You must make a commitment to grow consistently and never settle into a no-growth pattern.

Consistent growth requires confidence, and confidence only comes from the experience of successful attempts.

There is no better place to experience successful attempts than in the choice of accountability.

When you choose accountability, you must make a commitment to do what you say you are going to do and report on that to an outside partner on a weekly basis. During this process you will experience success and failure. It becomes a weekly proving ground for your commitment.

As you learn from this weekly choice of accountability, you begin to notice that you are doing things that you never thought possible. With time, you begin to understand this truth:

**You possess
an unlimited
amount of untapped
potential!**

When you become aware of this untapped potential, you begin to develop confidence in your potential. You become

---

FROM THE DESK OF MARK SMITH:

One big pitfall for many people is that they play the blame game. They blame others for their lack of success, their poor choices, their bad situations. Stop! Refuse to ever play the blame game again.

Right here, right now, are you willing to take personal responsibility for your actions? Are you willing to set goals? Are you going to identify your why, your motivator that will drive you and keep you on track? Are you willing to be coachable?

If you are, then you are on the road to becoming a high achiever.

aware that no matter how challenging the future may be, you have the untapped potential to successfully deal with it.

It is difficult, if not impossible, to develop this confidence in your untapped potential **without** choosing to be accountable to your goals and learning to make a commitment.

#3 — *Understand that accountability is a choice*

Accountability is a mature choice. Some say that accountability is a sign of weakness. These people try to achieve in private with a false sense of independence and pride. They may reason, "I only need me, and I can account for myself better than anyone."

I have known only a few people who could do this on their own, and I would never recommend it. **For all next-level growth and every next-level step I have made in my life, the choice of accountability played a major role.**

Most of us need the outside perspective of accountability to grow, and in most cases, no one can make that choice for you. Forced accountability will produce only temporary results.

Choosing accountability is an effective choice because you cannot hide behind your comfort zones. Accountability **pushes you past those self-imposed limitations** and **into a lifestyle of achievement and growth**, which is what you want!

When you step forward with the choice of accountability, you are saying YES to achievement and growth.

Notes to Self:

_____

_____

_____

_____

_____

_____

_____

_____

_____

_____

_____

_____

_____

_____

_____

_____

_____

_____

_____

_____

_____

_____

PART II

Using a Proven System to Succeed

We have devoted the first half of this book to the discussion of learning to make effective choices. You are therefore aware that the management of effective, daily choices like positive attitude, effective actions, and the choice of accountability, are not natural responses.

In order to be consistently effective, you must have ...

**a consistent system,
exclusive of your own instincts,
to manage your daily choices and actions.**

The remaining chapters are intended to serve as your personal guide to the Next-Level Achievement System®.

Chapter Five

The Next-Level Achievement System®

In this chapter, we will begin building the foundation of an effective personal management system. For over 20 years, I have personally used and helped thousands of leaders learn an effective system that I call the Next-Level Achievement System®.

Regardless of what you may be thinking, please approach this system with an open mind. It is time proven, and it works incredibly well. You have my word on that!

There is only one purpose for this Next-Level Achievement System® ... **to bypass your natural, human instincts**.

Remember:

> **Your human instincts**
> **are only interested**
> **in your comfort and safety,**
> **and their #1 goal is to keep you**
> **where you are.**

That is why change is usually uncomfortable.

When you develop and use a system that is designed to keep you focused on what matters most, you **bypass** those **nagging comfort zones** and **systematically move toward goal-directed achievement**.

Fighting change

Have you ever attended an inspirational or motivational event and come away with great intentions to change, only to find yourself back to your old habits within just a few days?

Good intentions must be supported by effective choices.

Every year, fitness centers across the US are overwhelmed by new registrations in January from people who genuinely want to become physically fit. They have good intentions that are backed by New Year's resolutions, but by March, most of these new registrations have cancelled.

Why are good intentions not enough to generate change?

Good intentions must be supported by effective choices, and that is where most people go astray. Achievement happens moment by moment, one day at a time! Many people have difficulty translating their good intentions into goal-directed, daily choices and actions. They don't realize this truth:

> **Good intentions are under the direct control of your natural, human instincts.**

Without an effective management system, which keeps your choices in alignment with your goals, **your comfort zones and habits of thought will take over**. That is why a personal management system is vital in achievement.

You cannot become who you have never been by doing what you have always done. Positive change is the key to achievement, and your effective daily choices are the stepping stones.

The 4 elements of the Next-Level Achievement System®

Simplicity is the key to a successful system of achievement for any leader because a simple system can be duplicated by others. Group energy is generated from the use of a common system within any group, large or small. Then, from a consistent system of achievement, a common language and a synergy of teamwork is spawned.

I will briefly discuss each of the elements of the Next-Level Achievement System® here, but the following four chapters will describe each of these elements in greater detail.

ELEMENT #1 — A vision statement

Your vision statement should be less than one page and should be written in present tense. Begin by writing a description of your life 5 to 10 years in the future as if you are already there. You should be somewhat realistic, but be careful not to limit your potential. This statement will be the foundation for all your future planning.

A part of your vision is a statement of your life's mission/ purpose. This mission/purpose statement will be remembered monthly in your personal management system. Your mission/purpose statement should describe your best self and define your heart and soul. Be patient, because a good mission/purpose statement may take years of refinement.

ELEMENT #2 — Annual goals

At the beginning of each new year, set 3 to 5 annual goals that will move you closer to your vision. These goals will be, and should always be, determined by and based upon your vision.

From these 3 to 5 goals, you will create action steps that outline what you need to do to accomplish these goals.

ELEMENT #3 — Monthly plans

The action steps from your annual goals should filter down to your monthly plans. You will need a month-at-a-glance

FROM THE DESK OF MARK SMITH:

Your vision statement is a subliminal message that you send to yourself. The vision statement may seem tedious at first, but it predicts where you are going. That is why it's so important.

In the process of creating your vision statement, you go through a lot of self-talk. You decide what you want this year, in a few years, and in all areas of life. This self-talk is what brings it all together.

Do you want a positive expectancy? Do you want a minute-by-minute, successful mindset? Do you want to get the negative seeds out of your mind?

A vision statement will do that. It keeps you focused and keeps distractions out. And in the process, you are reassuring yourself of your success.

Make the time to write your vision statement!

calendar for this. All target dates from the action steps of your annual goals, along with all scheduled events, should be entered into your monthly calendar.

ELEMENT #4 — Daily actions

Each day of your monthly plan should transfer to your daily actions, one day at a time. These daily plans will include imperative/important things to do, contacts and follow-ups, and a time schedule of your day.

The key to daily planning is to **always** plan tomorrow before tomorrow begins.

You may be thinking, "Wait, I didn't get all that you said!" That is fine. The next four chapters will be devoted to explaining in detail each of these parts of the Next-Level Achievement System®.

Planning is required

Achievement happens moment by moment, one day at a time! Effective daily choices come from a systems approach to pre-planning and daily management. **Becoming a master of daily planning is also a significant winner behavior you must develop.**

One of the most commonly asked questions that I get from clients is, "How can I achieve and still maintain balance in my life?"

We want to have it all, but can you have it all and still be balanced? I believe that a balanced life of abundance is achievable. My consistent answer to this question is, **"You can have it all if you commit to becoming a master planner!"**

FROM THE DESK OF MARK SMITH:

To back up your vision statement, you need daily affirmations. These affirmations are part of your self-talk, providing you with a bulletproof vest in the war zone of negativity around you.

Go into the coffee room of corporate America today with a big smile on your face — and watch the reaction of the room. They will ask you, "What's up with you?" They will think something is wrong. In the coffee room, they aren't asking you where you are going, what your dreams are, or why you have positive expectancy. No, it's all negative. It's about bad marriages, the boss, work, cars, loss, unfulfilled dreams, etc.

How can you be a high achiever in a negative environment? With self-talk and affirmations, you can excel past those around you. Write down your affirmations; then repeat them. Maybe you write "Get out of debt" or "Go to my children's events" or "Do whatever it takes to do it" down on a piece of paper.

When I was starting out as an entrepreneur, I was in the military and working 50-70 hrs a week, we had a newborn, and we were $40K in debt. What got me through were my daily affirmations.

I had a pocket full of index cards, and I read them all the time. My car had affirmations stuck all over the place, and at red lights I would read them. My mirror in my bathroom was covered with affirmations. Honestly, what do you want to see in the mirror, yourself or where you want to go in the future?

Here's one of the affirmations that meant a lot to me: "I will sacrifice my spare time so I'll have abundance."

Write your own affirmations, words that compel you to keep going toward your dreams. In the achievement process, you have to remind yourself daily of where you are going.

And it goes without saying that you do not ask anyone in the coffee room for advice.

Here it is:

A) If you want abundance, then you must have achievement and balance, and

B) If you want achievement and balance, then you must have a system of personal management that consistently brings your focus to the moment-by-moment, one-day-at-a-time process of effective actions.

Quite simply, you cannot have abundance without your system of personal management.

Prior planning helps you to become proactive against the comfort zone of procrastination.

To grow, you must overcome ineffective behaviors, and that requires the implementation of new, more effective behaviors. **Replacing old habits with new habits requires a system that stimulates behavior change.**

And again, behavior change *without* an external, consistent system would be difficult, if not impossible.

The desired personal habit of daily management is to plan first and act second.

You should always have your monthly plan ready before the month begins — and your daily plan ready before each day begins.

Prior planning helps you to become proactive against the comfort zone of procrastination. **Comfort zones rush in to fill the vacuum left by unplanned months and days.** Your system keeps you goal directed by pre-planning, and you simply act **rather than renegotiate** with your comfort zones.

Your best plans and intentions are worthless unless you assume personal responsibility and develop the capacity to mange your effective choices. In other words, simply do what you plan to do without hesitancy, regardless of circumstances or what other people say, think, or do.

FROM THE DESK OF MARK SMITH:

Another reason why a vision statement and a clear mental picture are important is that for most people, they don't know where their time goes.

That's how life is. Things go by so fast. I sit down and look at someone's activity report or planner and see how fast the time has gone. It's unclear to the person trying to achieve. "What have I done?" they ask.

It has little to do with skills and abilities and everything to do with the missing daily plan and missing written focus. Without those, people are aimless.

Those who are coachable can learn it, and they do. That is why your long-term success is found in your daily routine.

Notes to Self:

_____
_____
_____
_____
_____
_____
_____
_____
_____
_____
_____
_____
_____
_____
_____
_____
_____
_____
_____
_____
_____
_____

Chapter Six

The Vision Statement

Clarity creates focus! The clearer the vision (mental picture) of your future, the more focused your daily activities will be.

Maintaining consistent, **daily focus is vital for achievement**, and focus is a significant factor in the **sustainability** of that achievement.

Riding the wave up ... and then down?

It is not uncommon to watch someone achieve a level of great success, only to see them decline shortly thereafter. Why is that?

The answer to that question goes back to the basic problem we all have with achievement — **comfort zones** designed and built by our natural, human instincts.

After we reach a new level of achievement, there is a tendency to revert to our comfort zones. We rationalize this behavior by saying, "I just need a break." **The real meaning**

71

of that comment is, "I am so far from my comfort zone that I choose to go back there for awhile."

There is absolutely nothing wrong with a well-planned break for rest and to re-energize. However,

a WELL-PLANNED BREAK
vs.
a RETREAT TO AN OLD COMFORT ZONE
are two completely
different
issues!

The danger of retreating to old comfort zones is that you cannot sustain consistent growth by going back to old habits and behaviors. As soon as you retreat to an old comfort zone for rest, you lose momentum. **This dysfunction is caused by lack of focus.**

As soon as you retreat to an old comfort zone for rest, you lose momentum.

With clear focus, a well-planned break can propel you to higher achievement. But that is not the same as dropping back to a comfort zone of "no-growth."

The instant you revert to old habits and comfort zones, all growth stops, and as you know, there are only two growth choices in life: grow or decline!

The value of vision

Our human design includes a unique and creative gift ... **the gift of imagination**. We are the only part of creation with this unique gift. The ability to use our imagination to **envision a future as you want it to be** is the key to daily focus.

FROM THE DESK OF MARK SMITH:

High-level achievers take time to recharge their batteries. To sustain a high level of achievement, you also need to make plans for recharging.

I recommend that every 90 days or so, after running at 100%, that you reward yourself in some way. It's a small win in the formula for success. Build your success on back-to-back 90-day cycles. Run flat out, with good plans, focused on your goals and vision, but when you know rewards are coming, it helps you to stay focused. You know there is a rest stop along the way. Even the best car racers need a pit stop for new wheels, gas, breaks, etc., and so do you.

As my wife and I map out our 90 day cycles, we schedule in a 2-4 day "rest and reward" stop. We map it out. (We are not talking about taking a week or month off!) And we engage our whole family in the rest stop. I am focused on my goals, but knowing that on the 91st day I will be spending some quality time with my wife and kids feels good.

During those 2-4 days, shut off your phone. Do whatever is important and relaxing to you. You need to take a break to recharge yourself. You can't take the work out of work. Success and work go hand in hand. They go together, but you can make work fun and rewarding.

Schedule out your 1-5 year goals with established breaks every 90 days. During each 3-month cycle, you can remain laser focused and not have to worry about missing the fun things. When you do get your reward, it'll be the best 2-4 day break ever. You will have earned it!

A couch potato doesn't deserve a break, but you do. Get refreshed in those 2-4 days, find your second wind for your business and achievement plan, and crank out your next 90 days. This is how I create my roadmap to achievement.

When you allow yourself to use your imagination to picture a future as you want it to be ...

a) you create clarity,

b) and future clarity

c) creates focus for the moment.

This is why I place vision at the very beginning of my work with clients. The Next-Level Achievement System® rests on vision as the cornerstone of the entire foundation for the system.

Some of us have been conditioned by culture and education to believe that the use of our imaginations is an **inferior** and **wasteful** form of thinking. I remember several well-meaning but ill-informed teachers in my childhood who told me, "Stop daydreaming and pay attention."

FROM THE DESK OF MARK SMITH:

To be a high achiever, you need a superstrong vision. If your vision or why doesn't make you cry, then it isn't strong enough.

I tell people all the time, "It's mind over matter. If you don't mind, it don't matter." If you don't worry about it, it doesn't affect you. You move on. You don't make it into a big deal.

When you have a vivid goal in mind (i.e., better health) and you are sold on it, then you will break every barrier that tries to get in your way. No negative, no curve ball, and no person will be able to stop you.

Successful people have the same challenges as everyone else — but they handle the challenges differently because they have a vision that carries them through.

From this all-to-common type of negative conditioning, we develop resistance to the use of our imagination. We begin to think of daydreaming as wasteful.

In fact, the act of considering your vision as a process can actually be painful for certain personality types. Those who can only believe in what exists as current reality will say things like, "I believe in what I can see or touch." As a result, they have an additional resistance to an appreciation of imagination as a significant and creative thinking process.

Your vision statement is never about reality; it's about designing life by your dreams.

Is that you? If so, I suggest that you change your thinking about the gift of imagination.

Over the years, I have experienced all types of resistance to the process of vision, but the beneficial effects of using the imagination in the creation of a long-term vision is a significant factor in the system of achievement. **The real value of vision is that it puts the WHY behind what you do!**

Building a vision statement

I find that the most common practice of building vision is to simply list the things you may want in your future. A list of future wants is a good place to start, but that is a "Dream List," and I will cover that in the next chapter on goals.

A meaningful vision statement is much more than just a list of future wants. **A passionate vision statement actually propels you into your future with a vivid mental picture that includes sights, sounds, colors, feelings, and emotions.** A well-prepared vision statement will inspire both your feelings and your emotions.

75

STEP #1 — Pick a date in the future

The best way to get started building your own vision statement is to pick a future date (many people choose their birthday) five years into the future.

Now, with that date in mind, write down all the facts that would relate to your life at that time, such as your age, ages of the members of your family, home, location, or activities.

STEP #2 — Define your future

Next, think about the future facts and relate those facts to fit exactly what you want your life to look like in five years. You are defining your future as you want it to be.

STEP #3 — Write it out

Once you have your thoughts in place, write a narrative description of a day in your life, five years into your future. Design your narrative exactly as you want it to be.

Here is the key: **Write your narrative in the present tense as if you are already there.**

Your vision statement should be no more than one page long and should evoke strong feelings and emotions when you read it. There is something about building your vision statement into a description of a day in your life that brings your vision to life with all the sights, sounds, and feelings of reality.

STEP #4 — Post it so you can read it often

When you have your vision statement ready, type it up on your computer and put it into a format that you want. Then

FROM THE DESK OF MARK SMITH:

Having a clear mental picture is necessary in all areas of life. I'm an avid marksman. I was a coach in the Marine Corps, and for months, we did nothing but shoot. We'd start shooting at dawn, take a lunch break and shoot until dark. We did this every single day for three straight months! Why? To ingrain a clear mental picture.

Then, regardless of the circumstances, we were able to hit our target. Any good marksman, competitive shooter, or sniper in armed forces or police force knows that it's about having a clear mental picture. You actually see it happening before you even pull the trigger.

How do you hit a target that is so far away, you can't see it with your naked eye? You know your abilities, you know your gun, and you can do it because you've done it so many times before. You go through the mental process ... the rifle is a part of your body ... you feel every breath ... and you imagine the bullet coming out and going down range and hitting the bull's-eye. You have blind faith that it will hit.

Then you line up your sights, and with your clear mental picture of your shot, you squeeze the trigger. You envision it hitting right where it hits. It's almost an out-of-body experience! I've seen 100s of bull's-eyes in a row from those who are good at it, with incredibly minor variations.

But if you don't have the experience and lack a clear mental picture, you'll be concentrating on steering your rifle, getting the sights lined up, and hoping you'll hit the target.

The person without a clear mental picture is at an extreme disadvantage. I resolved that it would never be me.

Whatever you are aiming at, whatever goal you are pursuing, you need to have a clear vivid picture. You need to envision what you want and put it in front of you. Then it's a natural, fluid motion as you line up and go after it.

frame it and place it in a location where you will see it often.

Remember that your vision statement is never about reality. It is about designing life by your dreams. You only have two choices regarding your future:

**You can plan it
the way you want it to be,
or you can wait for the situations
and circumstances of life
to design it for you.**

Your vision statement should grow as you grow. Every year you will review your vision statement and update it as you see fit. **Your evaluation should always be how compelling your vision is, not how realistic it is**.

In the next chapter, you will learn how you can derive your annual goals, which will be very specific, measurable, and realistic, from your vision statement.

Get started and stop worrying about how perfect it will be.

Every year, you will ask yourself, "What can I accomplish this year that will move me closer to my vision?"

That is how specific annual goals act as stepping-stones to your vision of tomorrow.

The power of vision

Long-term vision is the key to energy, focus, and consistency. Clarity of vision acts as a magnet, **for you attract to yourself that which you set out for yourself.**

With clear vision, you can recognize opportunity when it presents itself because it fits the vision that you have carefully designed and clearly pictured for your future.

Without vision, people become:

listless,
    restless,
        scattered,
            fearful,
                pessimistic,
                    negative,
judgmental,
    short-sighted,
        burned-out,
            frustrated,

FROM THE DESK OF MARK SMITH:

If you don't have a plan, you plan to fail. Everyone is on the school bus of life. You can be a passenger or the driver. As long as you are on the right bus, you may get to the right place — but I don't want to bet on that. The bus will get you from A to B, but I want to get to B on my terms, in my time frame.

When I'm not the driver, someone else is. That person may take detours. They may go in circles. Either way, you are stuck. My personal view is this: You want to be the driver!

How do you trade places and get in the driver's seat? You have to unbuckle the comfortable seat belt and get up and ask the bus driver for permission to drive. You will gain more responsibility, and that may be uncomfortable, but you will have the lead at that point, and you can go where you want to go!

Choose to be uncomfortable and choose to lead. In doing so, you are choosing to win.

one-sided,
unbalanced,
depressed, and
discouraged.

That is a pretty sad list, but it describes many of our friends, family, and acquaintances.

I have experienced each of these dysfunctions with past clients, but I have also experienced many of those clients enthusiastically declare that clarity of vision was the key to their process of pushing past their mental dilemma.

Solomon said that, "Without vision people perish," and I have observed this to be true. I have numerous examples that prove him right. I have found that almost every case of executive burnout can be resolved with a process of building a passionate vision of the executive's future!

Vision is the foundation of the Next-Level Achievement System®. **You will never regret the time and energy invested in building a passionate vision of your future.** It is not easy, but it is not impossible.

Get started and stop worrying about how perfect it will be. Life is not about perfection — **life is about progress**. Building a passionate, compelling vision statement is one of the most significant requirements of next-level growth.

Notes to Self:

_____

_____

_____

_____

_____

_____

_____

_____

_____

_____

_____

_____

_____

_____

_____

_____

_____

_____

_____

_____

_____

Chapter Seven

The Goals

I remember my mentor, Paul J. Meyer, saying, "If you're not achieving at the level you want, it is simply because your goals are not clearly defined." He always focused on achieving goals, not just setting them, and he insisted that the difference was in the process.

Anyone can set a goal, but **achieving the goal** is the true purpose of goal setting.

Set only a few big goals every year

"The Goals" section here is the second part of the Next-Level Achievement System®. Clearly defined goals serve as your directional compass and drive your effective actions and choices during the year. **Goals turn dreams into reality in small, annual increments.**

Each new year, you need to set specific, realistic annual goals. Those goals are always directed from your vision and dreams.

Begin by asking yourself, **"What specific goals can I achieve this year that will move me closer to my vision and dreams?"**

I recommend that you limit your goals to 1 to 5 big annual goals. The reason I suggest a limit is that the process will require a plan of action for each goal, and the tracking process required is quite involved. Too many goals will distract your focus from the achievement of the most important goals.

As an example, I once had a meeting with a CEO of a major organization. At the beginning of our conversation he said, **"I don't believe our company has a need for any further organizational planning because in three annual planning meetings, our team has established 152 corporate initiatives for the year!"** He beamed with pride.

We proceeded to discuss other issues, but during my remaining time with him, I was thinking to myself:

**"This well-intentioned leader
is totally unaware
of what he has done
to his leadership team."**

He was treating a glorified to-do list as if the 152 corporate initiatives were strategic goals. With this mind-set ...

**he had inadvertently set a
SELF-DEFEATING path of frustration
and a WASTED YEAR
of non-goal-directed work.**

Don't let that be you!

What happened to my goals?

My experience with leaders like this is that they tend to overwhelm their leadership teams with to-do's and call them goals. At the end of the year, they make excuses for why they did not hit the "goals" and set almost the same "goals" again for the next year.

What they are missing are the **clearly defined big goals that will move them closer** to their long-term vision.

Nobody can maintain consistent daily focus on vague, undefined goals.

In the absence of the clearly defined goal, **initiatives lose their meaning and significance**. Organizational leaders cannot maintain consistent daily focus on vague, undefined initiatives — and neither can you!

So, the initiatives lose their importance, and the function of simply **being busy begins to occupy the focus** of the entire organization. I have noticed that this happens to individual clients as well.

Willingness to work hard is important, but hard work alone does not necessarily lead to achievement.

FROM THE DESK OF MARK SMITH:

Are you willing to tell others what your goals are? Most people are hesitant, but if it's a real goal that you really want and expect to achieve, then you won't mind telling everyone about it.

You must proclaim the goals that you set for yourself. You need to tell your family, friends, and coworkers. When you make goal setting that vivid, you go a lot further.

I challenge you: If you are really serious about achieving your goals, proclaim it to everyone as you move forward.

Remember this:

"It's not how much you do,
but the effectiveness of
WHAT you do
that truly counts!"

Laser focus on specific, predetermined annual goals is the only path to effective work.

Real goals represent those few and specific, all-inclusive, important, annual achievements necessary for consistent progress toward your long-term vision and dreams. The "strategic initiatives" that seem to occupy traditional corporate thinking are usually the **action steps** to the big goals.

But goals are not action steps!

IDENTIFYING real goals and ...

> **RECOGNIZING the differences between goals and action steps ...**

> **are the MAGIC INGREDIENTS ...**

> > **to the process of successful goals achievement.**

I would recommend that you re-read those words several times to let this truth settle in. Most people, including CEOs, do not recognize this important truth.

Identifying your goals

From my past years of experience and observation, I am now convinced that **there is a simple reason** why most people do NOT achieve the goals they set. **Are you ready for it?**

It is simply because ...

**people tend to set goals
that they really
do NOT want
to achieve.**

Anytime I use that comment in a group setting, I see both **shock** and **disagreement** in the faces of my audience. The obvious question in their demeanor is, **"How can you say that people set goals that they don't want to achieve?"**

Well, here are two examples to which I believe everyone can relate:

> **First, have you ever set a New Year's resolution?** It feels so good when you do it. It even brings a fresh newness to life and a genuine feeling of beginning anew. That is ... for about a week. Your behaviors never change to come in alignment with your goal, and by March, you say to yourself, "I'll get around to that next year."
>
> **Second, have you ever set a weight loss goal?** Did you achieve that goal? Now I know that some of you can answer that question with a resounding affirmative, but the majority of people who set weight loss goals never achieve them. Why is that?

Be honest with yourself: *Are you pursuing a goal that you really do not want to achieve?*

The answer to both the failed New Year's resolutions and the unattained weight loss goals is the same:

**Your behaviors
NEVER CHANGED
to come in alignment
with your goal!**

Ouch! A good measure of reality sometimes hurts. But learn from your lessons so you can avoid repeating the same mistakes.

Here is why: Any time you set a goal and your behavior does not change to come in alignment with the appropriate actions necessary to accomplish the goal, **you have psychologically determined that you do not want to achieve that goal**. And once you subconsciously decide that you do not want what the goal represents, regardless of the work effort, **you will not accomplish the goal**.

This is why identifying the appropriate goal is so important.

In the first part of the Next-Level Achievement System®, you started the goal setting process with the building of your long-term vision. **A clear mental picture of your ideal future is the first step in goal setting.**

Another necessary part of identifying appropriate goals is the building of a Dream List, which is a list of all the things that you ever wanted to have, do, be, and all the places you ever wanted to go. **Dreams are not goals, but they are the beginning of goals.**

We do not have room here to write your list, so take a notepad and begin to write down everything that comes to mind.

As you build your list, try not to be judgmental about whether the dream is realistic. If it is in your head as a want, write it down. This will be an ongoing list, hopefully for the rest of your life. Continue to add to your list as often as you

FROM THE DESK OF MARK SMITH:

Your goals need to be in front of you every day, and not just in print. You need pictures! Whoever said a picture is worth a thousand words was absolutely correct.

You need a "dream board." Go get a 2x3 foot foam board. Then cut out things important to you. If you want to go on a family trip, then get the brochure and put it on the board. Lastly, hang it on the wall somewhere that you'll see it every day.

If you have a financial goal, make one of those fundraiser thermometers; then fill it in as you grow toward your financial goal. You need a gauge to monitor your progress as you achieve your goal, whatever it might be.

If you are looking for a new car or house, don't put any old car or house photo on your board. Find the specific one you want.

Not long ago, I wanted a certain new car. I went on the website, I built the car online and printed it off. Then I got a screen saver of it on my computer. Then I went down to the dealership and test drove it so many times that they wanted to kick me off the lot.

Grab an empty jar, tape a picture of the car you want on the side of the jar, and capture the smell inside the new car. Then whenever you are tempted to give up the dream, you crack open the can and get a whiff of how your new car will smell!

After all, if you have no plan, you plan to fail.

think of new dreams, and put a date beside each dream as you write it down.

When I was moving to my new office in July of 2000, after being named President of Leadership Management, Inc. (I began with this company as a young man in 1978), I came across my old Dream List. I had to smile when I looked at #2 on my list from that year: "To become the President of Leadership Management, Inc."

A Dream List has a special, magnetic pull ...

> **It seems that you have a tendency
> to attract to yourself
> that which you
> set out for yourself.**

Lastly, keep updating your list of dreams. It is an important part of identifying your goals.

Where the goal setting process begins

The best time to set goals is the first of the year, but getting started is the most important step. So, get started now, regardless of the time of year. Then plan to use the last quarter of every year to establish your goals for the next year.

Here is where the goal setting process begins:

#1 — Review your vision statement

As you begin, start with a review of your vision statement. Your review should be about how compelling it is. If it has lost some of its luster, refine it. Your vision statement should grow as you grow.

#2 — Read through your Dream List

After you review your vision, read through your Dream List. Now ask yourself, "What can I accomplish this year that will bring me closer to my vision and dreams?"

The answers to this question are the beginning of your annual goals program.

#3 — Choose your top goals

As you write down the things you want to accomplish this year, try to identify which of those things are primary and which things are systemic. In other words, decide which things are the primary goals and which things are the results of the accomplishment of the primary goals.

As an example, say you wrote down these three things as goals for the year:

1. Earn $70,000 income
2. Increase savings account by $8,000
3. Buy a new home

On the surface, this list looks like three separate goals, but in reality, the list represents **one primary goal** and **two systemic benefits**. All three things are related to the financial area of your life and without the income of $70,000, the savings increase and the new home purchase are in jeopardy.

So, what you have is the one goal to earn $70,000 income and the increased savings and new home purchase are two benefits to be gained by reaching your goal.

Identifying the real goal is very important. By identifying the right goals, you can now work on your action plan with confidence.

Taking action on your goals

Once you have set the goals you want to pursue, deciding on your top goals, it is time to put an action plan together. The action plan is the lifeblood of goal setting, for **a goal without an action plan is merely a wish!**

There are three parts to the action plan:

PART #1 — Benefits to be gained and losses to be avoided

Write down all the personal benefits that the accomplishment of the goal represents to you.

Next, ask yourself, "In the pursuit of this goal, are there any losses that I need to avoid?" As an example, if you set a financial goal, you may wish to avoid the loss of relationships or integrity.

A goal without an action plan is merely a wish.

People are usually motivated by either the **benefits to be gained** or **losses to be avoided**. It is important to go through the thinking process regarding these two considerations and record them with the statement of the goal.

PART #2 — Obstacles and solutions

There are obstacles to every goal you set, so identify as many as you can, write them down, and then write a corresponding solution to each obstacle.

You cannot proceed with a goal if you have an obstacle to the goal for which there is no solution. In this case, many times the obstacle replaces the old goal and becomes the new goal.

PART #3 — Specific action steps

Write down each separate action step necessary to the accomplishment of the goal. Make sure that each action step is very specific and not vague.

Each action step must have a target date for its completion, and the target date for each action step must be recorded in the appropriate monthly calendar. This assures that the action steps transfer to your monthly plans.

Your goals program

As you can see from this chapter, your goals program becomes the guiding directional compass for your year.

FROM THE DESK OF MARK SMITH:

You must have a written plan that includes SMART goals: specific, measurable, attainable, realistic, and tangible.

Once you have a written plan, the last and final step is execution. Most people get excited about a goal, whatever it is, and some even write their goal down — but very few execute it. Everything comes down to execution.

Myles Monroe brilliantly noted, "Your fortune is found in your daily routine." Time goes by so fast. A five-year block goes by in a snap of a finger. You can remember where you were back then, can't you? And it wasn't so long ago!

You must stay focused on the daily execution of your goals. That is why it all comes down to your daily method of operation.

Annual goals flow into your monthly plans by target dates. The action steps are then brought into action by your daily planning.

There are many nuances to goals achievement, but they are too numerous to cover here. However, I would like you to remember this: **The way to achieve your goals is to follow the Next-Level Achievement System®.**

By following this system, your vision and dreams slowly grow into reality. You move past being a mere goal setter and you become a master goals achiever!

Notes to Self:

Chapter Eight

The Monthly Plans

People often ask me, "How should I remind myself of my goals after I've set them?"

I believe the stimulus for this question relates to the old adage, "**Out of sight, out of mind.**" They are concerned, and rightfully so, that they will forget very quickly if they put their goals program aside and never refer to it during the year.

Keep goals in sight

This mistake has been demonstrated in my personal experiences with major corporations. I have watched organizations pay thousands of dollars for outside management consulting firms to design strategic plans.

You cannot hit goals in the dark.

Then when all the work is done, the leadership **places the plan on the shelf** and **only refers to it at the end of the next year** to see how close or far they came to the goals!

You can probably guess the results.

97

You cannot hit goals in the dark. Goals require plans and plans must become relevant on a monthly basis.

In order to remember your goals on a consistent basis:

**Your goals must have action steps
and those action steps
must flow, systematically,
into monthly plans.**

In addition:

**The target dates for the action steps
must stand out as a
time-scheduled event on
the appropriate monthly calendar.**

This is accomplished by the systematic process of monthly planning.

The purposes of monthly planning

Monthly planning has three purposes:

1) **To remind** yourself of "Who you are" with a Mission/Purpose statement that describes your very heart and soul,

2) **To identify** your top priorities for the month, and

3) **To organize** your time-scheduled events on a monthly calendar so that you can see it at a glance.

We will cover each of these purposes with the appropriate detail needed for you to implement effective monthly planning.

PURPOSE #1 — Mission/purpose statement

With corporate clients, I usually suggest the separation of the Vision, Purpose, and Mission as stand-alone statements representing the entire organization. But with individuals, I suggest combining the mission/purpose statements together.

Everyone should have a written mission/purpose statement. **The reason is that we all need to know, with complete clarity, WHO we are!**

If I were to ask you to tell me, in one sentence, who you are, **what would you say?**

Inevitably, people usually respond with a glowing advertisement about what they do ...

You have as much time as anyone else to reach your goals.

BUT there should be

a DISTINCTIVE difference

between WHO you are and

WHAT you do.

That is the very objective of an individual mission/purpose statement. The statement is a one-sentence declaration of who you are and should describe your very heart and soul.

I have found that good mission/purpose statements never just happen — they usually evolve over time.

Begin by writing a one sentence statement declaring who you are. The best way to do this is to begin the sentence with the words "I am" and simply complete the sentence.

Your mission/purpose statement is for you and should declare who you are rather than what you do. It is not an advertisement for your services. Keep it about who you are not what you do.

As example, "I am an inspiring, caring and compassionate person" is a mission/purpose statement from one of my clients. The objective here is to keep it simple, a clear declaration of who you are.

Mission/Purpose Statement:
(I am ...)

_____

_____

_____

_____

FROM THE DESK OF MARK SMITH:

High achievers are always thinking 24 hours a day, but the body requires sleep and rest. For years, I had a tough time sleeping. My brain would keep on running, no matter how badly I needed my rest.

Now, I plan before I go to bed — and I sleep peacefully! By planning, the next day has shape, and I don't have to think about it any more. It has put me in almost a catatonic state. I already know what I need to do the next day. It's part of my achievement plan. I let my planner take me where I've already planned to go, and I go to bed.

The building block of "planning tomorrow before tomorrow begins" releases your mind and soul. Yes, curve balls come, but the planner keeps me on track. I have been able to accomplish far more this way than ever before, and though it sounds like a mattress commercial, I am sleeping so much better!

Even though it is only one sentence, this is some of the hardest work you will do. Just get started, and it will evolve into the real you as you remind yourself of your mission/purpose at the beginning of every month.

PURPOSE #2 — Identify monthly priorities

From the last chapter, you learned that the system leads you to clearly defined annual goals. Those goals have specific action plans with target dates, and those target dates are transferred to the appropriate monthly calendar.

Monthly priorities, then, are determined by the action plans and target dates that you establish.

In monthly planning, it is important for you to consider both personal and business priorities for the month. Ask yourself, "What important personal objectives do I have for this month?"

If you fail to plan both personal and business time, your work will expand to fill the unplanned time with nothing but work!

Too many people limit their planning to business only. **This practice leads to imbalance in your life.** Attention to both personal and business planning leads to a fulfilling and abundant life.

Often I hear clients make these complaints:

- **I just don't have enough time!**
- **It seems I never catch up!**
- **Work is never ending!**

Here are the facts: **You have as much time as anyone else.** The problem is that you are not planning. Work is taking up all of the available, unplanned time.

There was a writer of management practice who developed a theory about this very thing. His name was Parkinson and he developed "Parkinson's Law," which says,

> **"Work will expand
> to fill the time available
> for its completion."**

There you go — he nailed it!

If you fail to plan both personal and business time, your work **will expand to fill the unplanned time with nothing but work!**

If you want it all with balance between work, family, and all the other areas of your life ...

BECOME

a MASTER

PLANNER!

Now, once you have identified your personal and business objectives for the month, prioritize both lists. Then, from your priorities, select your top one or two personal and

---

FROM THE DESK OF MARK SMITH:

Despite all the success I've achieved in the military and as an entrepreneur, the Next-Level Achievement System® has taken me to a whole new level of achievement.

The Next-Level Achievement System® will put your goals on paper and turn your vision into reality. It will ensure that it happens, and that is amazing!

business objectives. **These top objectives are your priorities for the month.**

I have noticed that prioritization is difficult for high achievers because high achievers want everything to be a #1, top priority. As a result, **they overwhelm themselves with too many #1 activities, and they lose focus**, which eventually leads to burnout and frustration.

Prioritization is important. Something has to be number #1 something has to be #2, and so on. **Prioritization brings clarity, and clarity creates focus.**

By identifying priorities, it does not mean that you forget all the other monthly objectives. In fact, I suggest that you review your list weekly. But, prioritization does help you focus on those high payoff activities that propel you forward.

Always plan next month before the month begins.

From your priorities, write down those activities that hold the highest degree of payoff for you this month. Your monthly objective is to spend the majority of your time in your high payoff activities.

PURPOSE #3 — Organize your monthly calendar

Your monthly calendar is the place where you enter all time-scheduled events. It is important to **build the habit** of going directly to your monthly calendar anytime you need to schedule an event that has a date and time.

The reason I suggest this habit is to eliminate the possibility of double entry of a scheduled event and missing an important date. If you enter time-scheduled events in more than one place, such as a legal pad, journal, sticky notes, phone, computer, and a calendar, you will miss a scheduled date from the double entry. Build the habit of entering your time-scheduled dates in one place — your calendar.

At the beginning of each month, **make sure you fill in your entire schedule**, including work, personal, and family time. Review your calendar with others who need to know your schedule before the month begins.

If you do 70% - 80% of your work in the last half of a month, imagine how much you could do in a full month if you were fully engaged all month long!

This avoids conflicts of scheduling that come from lack of prior planning.

The #1 rule for monthly planning

You always plan next month before next month begins! Planning next month is a time-scheduled event at the end of each month. Professionals who develop this habit avoid the end-of-the-month syndrome.

The end-of-the-month syndrome goes something like this:

**You do 70% - 80%
of your most effective work
after the 15ᵗʰ of the month.**

The reason for this habit is that you have designed a comfort zone of retreat at the beginning of each month where you tell yourself, "I have plenty of time."

In your first-of-the-month comfort zone, you are ineffective due to your lack of focus, and that comes from lack of planning. **Remember, clarity creates focus!**

You probably have great plans for achievement, so as the 15th of the month approaches, you step up your activity. In a frantic flurry of activity, you desperately attempt to get a full month's work done in only 10 - 15 days.

Clients complain to me all the time, "I don't know why I do this to myself!"

The answer is this:

**They have developed
an end-of-the-month
SYNDROME
from a first-of-the month
COMFORT ZONE.**

If that applies to you, it is time to change that.

FROM THE DESK OF MARK SMITH:

If you have a big one-year goal, you obviously intend to accomplish your goal. But for most people not following the system, they psych themselves out to NOT achieve their goal. They talk themselves off the pitching mound.

The Next-Level Achievement System® allows you to be a big thinker and shoot for the stars. Specifically, we break the big goal down into 12 months. Now, the "big" goal is only 1/12th the size of what you originally stated.

Then you break that 1/12th down into 30 small daily plans of action to accomplish during a month. That's how the Next-Level Achievement System® ensures that you win.

Imagine hitting the ball out of the park every time at bat! You can do that when you use the Next-Level Achievement System®. Every pitch is a home run. You plan it out, and you do it!

Monthly planning is one of the cornerstones in the Next-Level Achievement System®. **Planning next month before next month begins** can change your life and your results.

Notes to Self:

_____

_____

_____

_____

_____

_____

_____

_____

_____

_____

_____

_____

_____

_____

_____

_____

_____

_____

_____

_____

_____

_____

_____

_____

Chapter Nine

The Daily Actions & Choices

The best way for me to explain the significance of daily choices and actions is to use an analogy.

Consider an automobile — not just any auto, but picture your favorite make and model. Imagine the new, shinny glow of the metallic color, the new car smell that envelopes you when you sit in the driver's seat, and the engine that purrs and revs with power.

Everything is perfect about this new car of yours except one thing: There are no wheels!

Well, maybe you can justify being happy with what you do have. I mean, the car is beautiful with its shiny color, it has a big powerful engine, and you cannot forget the new car smell.

No, it just will not work, will it? All the benefits are for naught. Why?

For the obvious reason: The wheels are the strategic part of the car that allows it to actually go places!

Your daily actions and choices **represent that strategic part** of the Next-Level Achievement System® that allows you to actually achieve and go places.

In short, your daily actions and choices are the wheels of your life!

You can talk the talk,

> **look the part,**

> > **have all the trappings,**

> > > **project the image,**

and all the things we do to keep from facing reality, **but if you do not do the right things consistently,** your system is unsustainable.

The power and freedom to choose

The power of choice is the very foundation of achievement. The quality of your daily choices and actions are **measured by their effectiveness.**

Daily planning is **the key** to how effective your choices and actions will be.

The power of choice is the very foundation of achievement.

Dreams transform into reality **in small, sometimes unrecognizable incre-ments.** To achieve and to make that achievement sustainable, you must build the habit of consistent daily planning. You have been blessed with the significant power and freedom to choose. Those goal-directed, consistent, daily choices are the **stepping-stones to your future.**

110

Always plan tomorrow before tomorrow begins

I believe the most effective choice you will ever develop is that of **planning your tomorrow before tomorrow begins**. This may seem like advice you heard as a child, but I am amazed **how few people** actually do it.

Many people have developed the habit of managing their daily routine by circumstance, situations, or ineffective activities. **They are being led instead of leading.**

For example, they start the work day by waiting for the first thing to happen. They do not know exactly what that will be, but **they assume** that something will **happen because it always does**. From that first circumstance, they move to the next thing, maybe a call, text, or email. But if nothing happens right away, they move on to a familiar and comfortable activity, like listening to some good music or surfing the internet, until something happens.

FROM THE DESK OF MARK SMITH:

If what you do as a leader, coach, businessperson, owner, entrepreneur, or teacher can benefit and grow by building on the success of others, then you absolutely must have a system that is duplicable.

All high achievers run at 100 mph with their hair on fire, but that is not duplicable. You must have a system in place that can duplicate if you want others to achieve their goals.

I call this a two-way street leadership approach. The quality of the process is enhanced because your people are being heard, their goals are being acknowledged, and they can integrate into the common goals because their own goals are being met.

You might be able to go 100 mph without a break, but your team can't keep up with you. With the Next-Level Achievement System®, your team can keep up with you, and that is duplication!

With this behavior, they complete their day with **ineffective results** related to their overall achievement.

Recognize the important fact:

> **This reactive style of**
> **daily management becomes**
> **a comfort zone and**
> **breaking that habit**
> **can be difficult.**

Planning tomorrow before tomorrow begins is the most effective way to overcome this reactive style of personal management.

Before the end of your day, take 10 minutes to plan tomorrow. There are three steps involved in planning tomorrow:

STEP #1 — Transfer forward

Transfer any action step, contact, or follow-up that has not been completed today over to tomorrow's action steps list. Incomplete action steps should always transfer forward to the next day until complete.

This habit will prompt you to get things done today because you know that you will have to transfer it to tomorrow.

STEP #2 — Make notes

Make a permanent note of any communication you need to pass on to others and the people with whom you need to communicate that information.

This frees your mind from the task of remembering, **which is a waste of the creative thought process**. You learn to maximize face time and phone time.

Simply remember to refer to your notes for the reminder of what you need to communicate every time you are with someone, in person or on the phone.

STEP #3 — Stay on schedule

Look at your monthly calendar and transfer your time-scheduled events from your calendar to your daily time plan. This simply keeps you on schedule.

If you are not in the habit of planning tomorrow before tomorrow begins, it will take some extra work and focus on your part. **Prior planning brings clarity, and clarity creates focus.** **Prior planning brings clarity, and clarity creates focus.** Prior planning and clarity are also necessities for success in any endeavor!

FROM THE DESK OF MARK SMITH:

Taped on my computer monitor, I have these words that I've taken directly from David Byrd:

#1 — Always plan the day before the day begins!

#2 — Live from your planner!

These two directives have revolutionized my ability to get things done.

Once you've done your goal setting, you know your "why," you have your top goals for the year, and you have your affirmations — nothing else matters but the day to day methodology. The daily method will make it happen!

Effective habits enhance performance, and planning tomorrow before tomorrow begins is the most effective habit you will ever develop.

Work your daily plan with an effective management tool

Whether you prefer to use manual planners or electronic tools, **the most important thing is that you use something rather than your memory**.

Our brains are most useful when we are being creative and solving problems, but when we use our brains for remembering important bits of information, such as when and where to go, we have rendered this vital resource less than effective.

Your daily management tool needs to be effective at reminding you of your schedule throughout your day.

**If you use a manual planner,
you must keep it with you
at all times and allow it
to guide you through your day.**

When you are at your desk, on the phone, or in a meeting, develop the habit of keeping the planner open in front of you as a stimulus to stay on time.

Use your brain to be creative and problem solve — not to remember what's on your calendar.

I have always used a manual planner simply because I find that writing stimulates clarity of thought and clarity of thought motivates action. I have not experienced that with electronic tools.

114

However, if you choose to use an electronic tool, make sure it does the following:

1) Allows you to track daily action steps along with your daily time schedule.

2) Allows you to transfer incomplete action steps to the next day, until completed.

3) Allows you to defer things to remember to tell others to a permanent place to remember for you. You want to free your thinking from too many things to remember

Successfully managing your daily choices and actions is dependent upon managing from a plan and not your natural instincts. Using an effective management tool **frees you** to simply work from your plan and **not renegotiate daily** with your habits and comfort zones.

Building effective habits of achievement

Daily management of your effective habits is the key to doing the right things consistently over a sustained period of time.

However:

**We naturally build
daily habits around
our comfort zones**.

If you look at your day, you will notice certain habits that are productive — and you will see habits that make almost no contribution to your future achievement.

115

Achievement requires growth, and growth requires change. You may readily accept that, but recognize this:

**Change will upset
your comfort zones,
and those habits
will fight your growth
every step of the way.**

I have clients ask me, "What should I do with these comfort zones that have grown into habits that are so hard to change?"

My answer is to "displace" the old habits, one at a time.

Displacement is a psychological term that references the replacement of an established habit for a more effective one. Old habits will NOT just go away. **You must push in**

FROM THE DESK OF MARK SMITH:

At some point, you have to decide what you want out of life, in all areas of life. Then you have to decide what you are willing to sacrifice to accomplish those goals.

When you have answered those two questions, you need a plan and a system that will help you reach your goals.

You can't accomplish your goals without your own motivation, but all the books, seminars, CDs, trainings, etc. won't help you be self-motivated.

Motivation comes from within, and high achievers have white-hot burning desire inside of them — and you can create the same white-hot, passion by following the Next-Level Achievement System®.

It's all about execution, massive action, and choosing to do it. Make that choice today!

---

the new habit to displace the old. It is like changing a glass of dirty water with clean water. You simply continue pouring the clean water into the glass of dirty water until the old, dirty water is displaced with clean water.

When you begin to implement some of these suggested habits of achievement, **you will be successful by continuously pouring on the new habit.** Every time you catch yourself off the system, **immediately** go back to your new, more effective habit.

Old habits do not just go away ... you must displace them.

Avoid going through the process of feeling bad or feelings of failure. Those thinking patterns are counterproductive to your progress. Just smile and go right back to the new habit.

Rest assured that these effective daily habits can be successfully implemented through the process of displacement within a very short period of weeks.

The effective choices and actions necessary for achievement come to us moment by moment, one day at a time. You cannot manage your daily routine instinctively without your instincts stepping in to protect you or guide you to an old comfort zone.

> **Effective, daily management must flow from a system that is based on YOUR long-term dreams and goals.**

The power of choice is a double-edged sword; it cuts both ways. Your daily choices will either **serve your natural**

instincts of habit and comfort — or **serve your desire for achievement**.

Gain control of your daily choices and actions, work to make them as effective as you possibly can, and you take control of your achievement and destiny.

Notes to Self:

_____
_____
_____
_____
_____
_____
_____
_____
_____
_____
_____
_____
_____
_____
_____
_____
_____
_____
_____
_____
_____
_____

Conclusion

Last thoughts

Years ago, in a private conversation, I had a noted author of management theory tell me his definition of "systems thinking." Here is what he said:

> **Systems thinking is demonstrated by mentally climbing above the fray of operations and looking at the entire system as a whole, while at the same time seeing all the individual parts in complete concert.**

I will never forget that definition because it parallels precisely the Next-Level Achievement System®. At the very foundation of the "whole" system are the "individual parts in complete concert."

Achievement is simply **doing the right things consistently over a sustained period of time**.

The "sustained period of time" comes to you moment by moment, one day at a time. **The quality of your daily choices and actions are measured by their effectiveness,**

and it is the quality of that effectiveness that determines the degree of your achievement.

Highly effective leaders achieve greatly while ineffective leaders deliver sporadic results and low quality achievement. The difference between these two groups is this:

the consistent

effectiveness

of their actions.

We have discussed the significance of a system of achievement, a system that buffers and separates your human instincts from the management of your process of achievement. Building this system requires a development process rather than just the accumulation of knowledge. Skill and performance are **knowledge-based**, while achievement and next-level growth are **process-based**.

The quality of your process determines the quality of your performance.

The seminar industry is filled with those who claim to improve performance levels. They approach this methodology with knowledge-based skills training, but it is my professional opinion, from over 30 years of experience, that **knowledge-based skills training without a proven development process is wasteful and ill-advised**.

You always have to remember:

**Performance quality
is directly related
to the quality
of the process.**

122

Skills training and a development process are NOT one and the same, as is evidenced by this fact that:

**Training is event-driven
while development is process-driven.**

Furthermore:

**Training is usually aimed at performance,
but development is aimed at the very core
of your process: your habits,
behaviors, conditioning, and comfort zones.**

FROM THE DESK OF MARK SMITH:

For most people, the bottom has to fall out of their lives before they get serious about their goals. People hit rock bottom, they lose their homes, they can't afford to eat, and they find themselves in incredibly hard situations.

Why is it that most of these people will come out fighting and go on to achieve things they never thought possible? They have an "I can do it" attitude, and they make it happen!

Backed into a corner, they come out charging. They were going through life, mediocre and normal, and then suddenly they are off and running! How? What happened?

The answer is that they developed a white-hot, burning desire to do something, and they did it.

We can all have whatever we want, but how badly do you want it? What are you willing to sacrifice to do it? Those who have gone through the fire are the ones who get it. It's not where you grew up or which college you attended or whether you finished high school. None of that matters after you read this book.

The only thing that matters is this: How bad do you want it? Are you willing to go through brick walls to get it? That's all that matters. Now, go get it!

Achievement is a by-product of the quality of your process, **not your performance**. I know this comment may raise some eyebrows in the human development industry, **but the quality of your process determines the quality of your performance**.

There is certainly a place for training in the enhancement of performance, but not in the absence of a development process.

Let the process you have learned here serve as the stepping-stone to your phenomenal success. And may God bless you and your journey of achievement!

Notes to Self:

From David Byrd

Notes

I sincerely hope that this book may serve as a guide for many who search for that next level in their lives and careers. If you believe that I may be of some help to you in your achievement journey, please contact me at:

davidbyrd@davidbyrdconsulting.com

Next-level growth usually requires an experienced outside-in perspective. I would be honored to share my experiences with you in your journey.

To learn more about what I do and how I help leaders take it to the next level, visit my website:

www.davidbyrdconsulting.com